Clams

0 11557 03058 7

Clams

How to Find, Catch, and Cook Them

Curtis J. Badger
Illustrations by Vladimir Gavrilovic

STACKPOLE
BOOKS

Copyright © 2002 by Curtis J. Badger

Published by
STACKPOLE BOOKS
5067 Ritter Road
Mechanicsburg, PA 17055
www.stackpolebooks.com

All rights reserved, including the right to reproduce this book or portions thereof in any form or by any means, electronic or mechanical, including photocopying, recording, or by any information storage and retrieval system, without permission in writing from the publisher. All inquiries should be addressed to Stackpole Books, 5067 Ritter Road, Mechanicsburg, Pennsylvania 17055.

Printed in the United States of America

Cover design by Caroline Stover
Cover illustration by Vladimir Gavrilovic

10 9 8 7 6 5 4 3 2 1

First edition

Library of Congress Cataloging-in-Publication Data
Badger, Curtis J.
    Clams: how to find, catch, and cook them/Curtis J. Badger; illustrations by Vladimir Gavrilovic.--1st ed.
        p. cm.
    ISBN 0-8117-3058-1
    1. Clamming. 2. Cookery (Clams) I. Title

SH400.5.C53 B34 2002
799.2'544--dc21   2001049892

Contents

Mercenaria: An Introduction

While this book is about clams, it is also about places where clams live. The hardshell clam (*Mercenaria mercenaria*) of America's East and Gulf Coasts prefers salt water, sandy beaches, tidal flats, salt marshes, and seaside bays. This I share with the clam. I, too, like these places, and perhaps that's why I'm partial to clams.

I've caught clams from New England to the Gulf states, in wilderness refuges and on tidal flats in the shadow of Manhattan skyscrapers. Clams, like people, are resourceful and adaptable. They can adjust to many situations. But to thrive, they need clean salt water, a bottom substrate of sand and organic material, vast salt marshes of *Spartina* and other grasses that provide life-giving nutrients, and a regular and gentle tidal flow to carry these nutrients to the flats and bay bottoms where the clams lie buried, ready to suck in their lunch through an incurrent siphon.

I do most of my clamming where I live, on the coast of Virginia, where, fortunately for me and the clams, some one hundred miles of seaside coastline remain today much as when Captain John Smith explored here in 1608. Eighteen barrier islands line the coast, as well as numerous inner islands that lie between the ocean beaches and the mainland. Most of these islands are protected through either federal or state ownership, and The Nature Conservancy's Virginia Coast Reserve is a sanctuary of about forty-five thousand acres on fourteen islands and the mainland.

This landscape is a delight for both clams and clammers. Here you can walk a wilderness beach for hours and see no other humans. You could paddle a canoe daily for a lifetime and still not explore all the bays and waterways. You can walk a salt marsh and see no buildings, no roads, none of the so-called improvements we classify as civilization.

It is important, I think, that we have such places and that we protect them so that our grandchildren and their grand-children will be able to enjoy the values of coastal wilderness as we do. Although the topography differs greatly, the wilderness landscape of the coast provides the same values as a wilderness in the American West or Alaska. There are too few places today where we can go to be alone in the natural landscape.

I find a day spent gathering clams on a remote seaside tidal flat restorative. The important thing about wilderness, whether on the coast or in the mountains of the West, is the effect it has on the human spirit. Hiking a wilderness beach is different from hiking a resort beach, or even a national seashore where development is held to a minimum. It has to do, I think, with the great value of seclusion, with places that are wild and remote and provide the illusion, if only for a few hours, of being untouched, of being as they were when they were created.

A wilderness beach is defiled by even a modest two-lane road, because the road destroys the illusion of remoteness. A single house on a remote island or salt marsh defiles it for the same reason; it reminds us of the sometimes stifling nearness of civilization.

So it's important to have wild places like these barrier islands, bays, and salt marshes. They make it possible for clams to thrive, and the clams give us an excuse to get out there.

The clams that we find here are locally called hardshell clams. In New England, they are known as quahogs (pronounced CO-hogs). The scientific name for the clam, *Mercenaria mercenaria*, was given because the clam was used in trade by Native Americans. The purple inner shell was polished and shaped into beads, and these were bartered for food and other goods. Today, the Wampumworks of Dunstable, Massachusetts, is a contemporary dealer in shells. The company fashions beautiful jewelry from *Mercenaria*, carving and polishing the shell and mounting it in gold or silver settings.

There are many other kinds of clams as well. Farther south on the Atlantic coast is found a clam called *Mercenaria campechensis*. Some consider it a separate species, but it interbreeds with *M. mercenaria*. Softshell clams or steamers, *Mya arenaria*, are popular among recreational clammers in New England. Surf or sea clams, *Spissula solidissima*, and ocean clams, *Arctica islandica*, both are harvested in the deep waters of the Atlantic Ocean. They are totally different genera than *Mercenaria*. Sea clam shells are sometimes found washed up on barrier island beaches.

This book focuses on *Mercenaria*, the favorite of recreational clammers throughout most of the coastal United States. These are clams of tidal flats, of shallow waters where they often can be found at low tide by locating their "sign." The clam burrows about an inch under the surface of the flat and feeds through a pair of siphons. These make holes in the surface, indicating that a clam is present. If you find no clam sign, you may still find clams by drawing a long-tined rake across the flat or along the bottom in shallow water. Clams can be found in a soft bottom by feeling them with the feet.

While gathering clams on a tidal flat is an enjoyable way to spend an afternoon, the real reward of clamming comes a few hours later in the kitchen. Clams are one of the most versatile types of shellfish we have and can be prepared in ways that are as simple as eating them raw on the half shell or steamed and dipped in melted butter. Clams go well with pasta. They are tasty fried singly or made into fritters. Clams can be cooked in pastry shells to make a dinner pie, and there are an endless number of clam chowder recipes, most of which reflect geographic ties.

So the intent of this book is to teach you how to find clams, how to catch them, and how to cook them. And in doing so, I hope it will give you a greater appreciation not only for clams, but also for the places where they live.

Curtis Badger
Onancock, Virginia

1   How to Find Clams

To catch a clam, you must first find it. This bit of wisdom may at first seem obvious, but I've spent many hours scratching and scraping tidal flats and finding nothing but worm holes. I finally learned that if one is to catch clams, one must think like a clam.

Well, that may be something of a stretch, since the clam has no brain as such. But the clam does have its needs. It wants water of the proper salinity. It wants tasty plankton suspended in the water column, but it doesn't want clay and silt and other inorganic material that will clog up the works. The clam is not exactly a social animal, but it's crazy about sex, especially when the water temperature begins to rise in the spring. Thus it wants a home where the spring warmth nudges the mercury into the erogenous zone. Then all the brother and sister clams cloud the water with eggs and semen, creating a protein-rich broth that the clam community, and many others, feed on.

So the clam wants a comfortable home, a ready supply of food tastefully presented, and unlimited opportunity to have sex. That's not too much to ask, I suppose.

When searching for good clamming areas, consider first the "comfortable home" portion of the equation. The clam lives just below the surface of the bottom, and it prefers a substrate it can dig into fairly easily. Mud works, as long as the water above it does not contain too much suspended material. Sand also works. But most clams prefer a combination of the two. They want a substrate that's firm enough to protect them from predators, such as clear-nosed skates, but easy enough to excavate.

On a recent clamming trip, I decided to do an informal analysis of a tidal flat that was especially good clamming ground. I dug my hand into the flat, finding it firm but malleable. I worked my fingers around shell fragments and reached a depth of about four inches. I then lifted a handful of the material, drained away the water, and placed it in a sandwich bag. The material was dark and mudlike, in that it clung together when I squeezed it into a ball, but the texture was fairly rough, indicating the presence of some coarse sand and shell fragments. I took it home, put it in a dish on the picnic table on the deck, and gave it a day to dry.

The dried material took on a lighter color, and when I fingered it, the grains separated like sand. As I spread it around the dish, I found a coquina in the mix, plus an oyster shell about an inch in diameter, a small mussel shell, a portion of a periwinkle, and numerous other unidentifiable shell fragments.

A 30X hand magnifier provided a closer view. Most of the crystals were light and glasslike, probably quartz. There were a few golden ones, perhaps feldspar, and many smaller black fragments that were probably a mixture of magnetite and bits of shell. Surprisingly, there seemed to be little organic material in the mix. So this tidal flat that is so popular with clams has virtually the same makeup as beach sand, at least in the top three or four inches. The crystals were smaller, the sand finer, but the composition was virtually the same.

This particular flat lies behind Metompkin Island, not far from a small inlet, but off the main channel that links the inlet with Folly Creek. On one side of the flat is deep water, and on the other is a salt marsh with a lush growth of *Spartina alterniflora,* one of the major food sources of the clam. A somewhat deeper area, perhaps eight feet wide, separates the flat from the salt marsh.

The tidal flow across the flat is constant, but not extreme, as it would be in a narrow channel. The presence of beach sand in the top layer of the flat indicates that the current does not have sufficient velocity to keep sand particles in suspension in an average tidal cycle, but there likely is velocity enough to keep lighter and smaller plankton suspended in the water, thus providing the clams their dinner.

The *Spartina* grasses grow tall and lush in summer, turn brown in fall, and in winter begin the process of decay in which the sun's energy stored in cellulose will be carried by the tides to the sandy flats, where it will give life to millions of clams and other creatures of this shallow lagoon.

So here on one of my favorite flats, the clam has perhaps an ideal geological composition for a home, the water is clean and moves properly, and there are many other clams in the neighborhood to ensure survival of the species. I can't imagine clams as social animals; I can't fathom them communicating with each other, but I rarely find solitary clams. If a tidal flat has clams, it has numerous clams, rarely just one or two, unless a storm or some other factor upset the normal life cycle.

Clams need others close by in order to reproduce. Here in this clam community, food is in plentiful supply, the salinity is perfect, and generations of clams live here, just as in a community of humans. The large clams are more than thirty years old and have probably lived their entire adult lives on this flat, within a few square meters of where they were found.

At that size, the clam has few predators, and it has been very fortunate to reach old age. Smaller clams are dug out of the bottom by crabs, skates, and rays, which crush the shells and feast on the animals inside. Larval clams feed a wide range of marsh creatures, including crabs, shrimp, fish, and birds.

Humans, too, are major clam predators. Like crabs and skates, we dig clams out of the bottom, pry open the shells,

and have the animals for dinner. Unlike crabs and skates, we've discovered various ways of finding clams and preparing them for dinner.

The fact that clams are filter feeders helps us find them. The clam hides by burrowing beneath the surface of the flat or bay bottom. Yet in order to live, the clam must eat and expel waste, and in order to further the species, it must engage in sex with other clams.

These things the clam does in a manner that is as anonymous as possible; the last thing it wants is to call attention to itself. So the clam uses two siphons, which it extends through the sediment in which it is buried to gain access to the water that covers the flat or bay bottom. It pulls in nutrient-laden water through its incurrent siphon, and it expels waste through the excurrent siphon.

An experienced clammer looks for the holes made in the tidal flat by clam siphons. Find the hole made by a clam, and you have found the clam itself. Thus clamming is an exercise in finding evidence of things not immediately seen.

The problem, however, is that many things make holes in tidal flats. A tidal flat, to the untrained eye, is a rather desolate landscape and not at all inviting. The flat, though, is awash

Relative size of razor clam, right, and mussel. Razor clams average four to five inches in length.

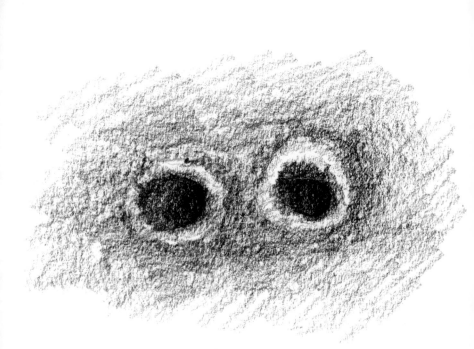

Clam sign.

with life at all tidal cycles. Dozens of species of boring worms drill into the surface of the flat. Snails, crabs, mussels, whelks, and many other small shellfish burrow into the sediment. Even the birds of the flats—willets, yellowlegs, and oystercatchers— bore into the surface of the exposed flats searching for prey.

So it takes some experience to become a good signer, to learn the difference between authentic clam sign and a worm hole. And to further complicate the situation, not all clam sign looks alike. Sometimes the holes are joined in sort of a keyhole shape. Sometimes they are well defined, and other times they are just the hint of a dimple in the sand. Sometimes you can find a hole with clam scat around it, providing irrefutable evidence of what lurks below. Clam scat is a brown, threadlike substance about one-eighth inch long.

If you're really lucky, you'll find the hole left by the excurrent siphon, and around which will be spatter marks in the sand left by the water expelled by the clam. This is best done on an early flood tide, after the flat has been exposed for some time at low water.

Find the hole left by the siphon, pull your clam pick or rake across the hole, and if fortune is with you, you will be rewarded with a chalk-on-blackboard squeak that means that a clam indeed is below the surface. All that remains is to pry it loose, pull it out, rinse it off, and add it to the basket.

If, for some reason, the clams have not been feeding or reproducing, they will not be making sign and are more difficult to find. Raking blindly across the flat often works, or you can wade in shallow water and feel clams in the soft bottom with your feet.

2   We Hunt, We Gather

A clam has only two goals in life: to eat and to have sex. Hence the phrase "happy as a clam."

Unfortunately, as the clam has no brain, it derives no real pleasure from either food or sex. The clam is a chemically driven shell full of salty flesh that exists to procreate. When she senses the presence of male pheromones, a mature female clouds the water with sixty thousand eggs, each of which may become a larva and eventually a mature clam.

Few succeed. The clam's remarkable fecundity serves not only to reproduce itself, but also to feed countless organisms in the seaside food chain. In spring, when rising water temperatures get the clams feeling frisky, the shallow waters of the seaside become rich with eggs and larvae.

Countless creatures forage on clams during the various stages of their lives. Small snails and shrimp feast on the tiny eggs and larvae. I prefer my clams a bit larger and more mature, littleneck size for steaming, or perhaps hefty old chowder clams for making a clam pie.

Our family went foraging last week, which means pulling on the hip boots and going out to a tidal flat at low tide to try to find something to eat. No, the pantry wasn't bare. Sometimes we want a dinner we hunted and gathered ourselves, not something that was raised in a factory, pumped up with hormones, and shrink-wrapped in plastic. Periodic foraging trips reinforce our presence in the food chain; they make us realize that humans are not above nature, but are of nature.

It was one of those rare spring afternoons when the sun shines gently, the breeze slightly stirs, and there's a compelling need to get out on the water. So my wife, Lynn, and son Tom and I loaded the skiff with clam picks and a wire basket, and headed out to a tidal flat in search of dinner.

Tidal flats are not colorful landscapes—I doubt whether Monet ever painted one—but they are remarkably full of life. Ribbed mussels burrow in colonies along the edge of the salt marsh, sort of a marine version of cave dwellers. Blue crabs scurry through the shallows, fiddlers bore holes in the sandy upper regions, and large channeled whelks burrow into the bottom mud. Shrimp forage in quiet pools, searching, as we were, for clams. Oysters cling to the remains of a long-abandoned boat dock. We were tempted to sample them, but considering their scarcity, we left them alone and wished them well.

And so, here we were in nature's own seafood department. What would we have for dinner?

We decided upon clams, beginning with a few tender littlenecks, about an inch and a half in diameter. We would steam them open and have them with melted butter. We might pick up a few mussels for the pot as well, and if we were fortunate enough to find razor clams, these would do nicely in the mix.

For our main course, we decided on linguine with clam sauce, a simple dish that avoids befouling these tasty morsels with tomato sauce or cream. We sauté chopped garlic until it becomes golden, and then we add chopped clams and their broth. We cook until the clams are just done, add a handful of chopped fresh parsley, and ladle the mixture over pasta. It gets no fresher than this.

But first we had to find them. For a creature with no brain, the clam has developed some extraordinary means of dealing with predators. The clam depends upon neither guile nor

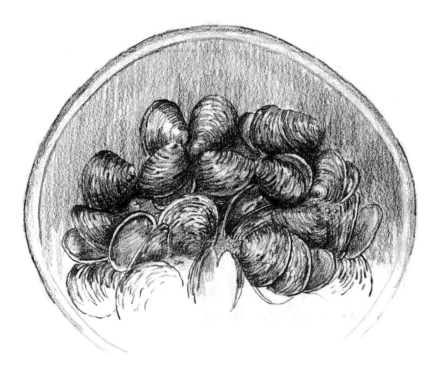

bravery when escaping enemies; it relies strictly on chemical reaction.

The clam avoids most predators by burrowing an inch or so below the surface of the tidal flat. A pair of siphons enables it to feed and expel waste. But when a clam senses danger, it will burrow a foot or more below the surface.

Mike Castagna, clam expert with the Virginia Institute of Marine Science, told me of an experiment they once did in an aquarium. Clams burrowed to siphonal depth in one aquarium, and then water was taken from a second aquarium holding starfish, a clam predator, and added to the clam aquarium. Reacting to the chemicals left by the starfish, the clams burrowed to a depth of a foot or more.

We arrived on our flat at low tide; the surface was exposed and drying in the sun. In six hours, the flat would be covered with two to three feet of water. We were looking for clam sign, those irregular holes left in the surface by clam siphons.

I found the first as I was stepping out of the boat. It was roughly the shape of a keyhole, and around it was a bit of waste that had been expelled in water through a siphon. I scratched across it with the clam pick, and the grating sound of metal on shell made the identification certain. I pried the

clam out with some difficulty, wiped away the sandy mud, and placed it in the basket.

By the time the tide had begun to come back in an hour later, we had enough for dinner and some to share with the neighbors. We put the clams in the freezer, and in about an hour, nearly frozen, they opened easily. We chopped them, put them in the pot with the garlic and olive oil, and had them over pasta.

There is something elemental about growing and gathering your own food. In the checkout line at the Food Lion, I rarely think about where my dinner comes from. But eating clams that I've hunted and gathered with my own hands, I feel that I know a little about their world, and I appreciate how their great gift of procreation benefits such a wide range of living things.

3   How to Catch Clams

The wonderful thing about clamming is that you don't have to spend a lot of money to enjoy the sport. You'll find no titanium-shafted clamming rakes in the pages of L. L. Bean. Your sporting goods retailer will not have expensive Nike clamming shoes. There are no clamming magazines to subscribe to, no nonprofit organizations whose noble goal it is to save the clam, and in most states you won't even have to write a check to the government for the privilege of gathering a few clams. Nor should you worry about the proper clamming wardrobe. Fashionable clamming attire usually resembles thrift shop discards.

All you need is a method to get out to the tidal flats, some old sneakers to prevent wear and tear to the feet, and some sort of implement to dislodge the clam once you find it. Many wildlife refuges on the coast allow clamming in tidal waters, and in many coastal communities you can drive or walk to public clamming areas. Here on the Virginia coast where I live, the bays and flats are fairly remote, and in most cases a boat is needed to reach productive clamming grounds.

It's best to use a tool to pry the clams free of their home beneath the flat. You could dig them out with your fingers or toes, but a large clam is remarkably tenacious and seldom comes willingly to the clam basket. By the time you gather sufficient clams for the chowder, you'll need to make an appointment with a manicurist.

When clams are found in soft bottom, they can usually be freed with the toes. In the process of evolution, humans have

become very ineffective at using the lower digits. Seasoned clammers, however, are second only to the primates in lower digital dexterity. A good clammer can pry that clam loose with the toes, scoot it over to the other leg, and use the toes to lift it up the leg until the hands can reach it.

Until you develop such ability, you will need a clam rake or pick to pry the clam loose and bring it to the basket. Rakes and picks are available in most outdoor shops in coastal communities. A garden rake could be used in a pinch, but a clam rake has longer tines, which make it easier to find clams and give you more leverage when prying the clam from the tidal flat. If you must select a clamming tool from the garden section, try a hand cultivator. These have three or four tines of the proper length, although the tool lacks the width of the rake.

A clam pick is a smaller version of the rake. A pick usually has two tines, and most have short handles. These were obviously designed by people who either were extremely short or had never actually been clamming. I have a clam pick made by a local waterman. It has the usual two-tine terminal hardware, but the handle is nearly four feet long, meaning that I don't have to bend over when I want to investigate whether that keyhole-shaped opening in the flat is actually the sign of a clam.

There are numerous methods of catching clams, although I must admit that the verb "catch" seems somehow inappropriate,

in that it implies a process of speed and dexterity, neither of which applies to the clam or necessarily to those who go in search of them. Clams, to be kind, are not exactly fleet of foot, and those of us who search for them, if viewed from a distance, would be considered plodders. We wander around the tidal flats with eyes downcast, leaning against our clam picks for support, now and then bending slowly to peck at the sand, retrieving a fat seaside clam for our basket.

What we are looking for is clam sign, the telltale holes left in the flat by the siphons, or a bit of clam scat, or perhaps the splatter of water around a hole when the clam last pumped out. Once the clam sign has been spotted, the pick is used first to confirm the presence of the clam, and then to pry it free of the flat. Clams usually burrow an inch or less beneath the surface, and so on a sandy tidal flat, the presence of the hard shell is easily picked up by the metal tines.

A second method is simply raking for clams without looking for sign. Raking clams is a sport for those who are strong

of back and, I'm tempted to say, weak of mind. It takes no skill or experience to rake clams, as long as you can find a flat or shallow waterway where clams are present. You simply pull the tines across the bottom until they scrape across a clam shell, and then you pry the clam free.

The temptation here is to put on my pompous jacket, to preach of the nobility of signing clams, as opposed to the unskilled and unwashed practice of raking them. It's like fly-fishing for native trout compared with fishing for carp with dough balls.

Actually, it's not.

There are times when, for whatever reason, clams do not make sign. They have not been eating or making baby clams, or perhaps the scent of a predator caused them to burrow deep beneath the surface. At times like these, the rake is your best friend, especially if you really need some hot clam chowder. Also, some of the best clamming areas are those that are covered by water at all tides, meaning that you can't see the sign even if it is there. So raking is the best method in this situation as well.

A third method of clamming is called wading, or treading. You simply wade in shallow water where the bottom is fairly

soft and muddy, and you feel the clams with your feet. It's best not to do this barefoot, because there are sharp oyster shells and other dangerous objects lurking about. Old sneakers work, but if the soles are thick, it's difficult to feel the clams. Water shoes work better and are lighter in weight and designed to get wet. Local watermen here on the Virginia coast used to make flannel slippers to wear when treading clams. The flannel gave their feet a measure of protection and allowed them to take advantage of the natural dexterity of their toes, so that they could free the clams and lift them at least high enough to reach with their hands.

Whether signing, raking, or treading, you will need something to put your clams in. A heavy-duty plastic basket will do, but most hardware stores in coastal communities have baskets made of galvanized steel designed specifically for clamming. These will not soon rust or corrode, are impervious to sunlight (unlike plastic), and are constructed in a wire-mesh fashion so you can wash the mud off your clams by sloshing them around in seawater.

When my father taught me to clam, we used an old wooden bushel basket suspended in a tire tube. If we were treading clams, or raking in shallow water, we would tie the basket and tube to our waist and pull it along with us as we clammed. The method worked perfectly for some time, but wooden baskets do not take kindly to regular immersions in salt water, and one day, when being lifted from water to boat, the basket bottom broke free, spilling its contents of a hundred or so hard-won clams back from whence they came. It was then that my father recognized the advantages of investing in professional-level clamming equipment, such as galvanized metal baskets.

C lams are one of the most important animals of the seaside estuary. They feed on plankton, converting to energy sunlight stored in salt marsh grasses such as *Spartina*. The grasses wither and die in the fall, and as they decompose, they become part of the nutrient-rich soup of the marsh called detritus, which feeds clams and many other organisms.

Clams are remarkably fecund. A mature female releases tens of thousands of eggs during a breeding season, and many of these become larvae. The eggs and larvae become part of the zooplankton of the salt marsh, providing a food source for many animals. The clams that survive to become adults also feed many marsh animals, from skates and crabs to birds and humans.

The life cycle of the clam is unique. For the millions of eggs and larvae that cloud the shallow tidal waters in the summer, only a few survive. But the ones that do can live for thirty or more years.

Throughout their life cycle, clams feed many creatures of the salt marsh. When the water temperature rises in the spring, male clams release semen through their feeding siphons. The semen, which contains pheromones, is spread over the flat by the currents and is ingested by female clams. The pheromones stimulate the females to release eggs, which they expel through their excurrent siphon. Each egg, supported by a gelatinous envelope, floats freely in the current until it is eventually attacked by spermatozoa. As the embryo develops in the first few hours of life, it becomes covered with tiny hairs, called cilia, which eventually tear apart the gelatinous capsule. The fertilized egg then floats along on the current as the larva develops.

The larvae float freely in the seawater, forming a vital part of the detritus-zooplankton soup of the estuary. After twelve to fourteen days, the larvae that survive begin their metamorphosis into seed clams. The shell thickens, and a gland develops that secretes a tuft of long, tough filaments, which the clam uses to anchor itself on the substrate. The tiny clam (0.3 to 0.4 millimeters long) does not burrow at this stage, but

Clam larvae.

wraps these threads around sand grains or shell fragments. The attachment is not permanent; the clam can release itself and move on to habitat more to its liking, should it prefer.

What the seed clam looks for at this point in its young life is water of the proper salinity and a bottom that will be a good home for the adult clam. Clams grow best in seawater that contains from about twenty to thirty-five parts per thousand of salt. In fact, a larval clam will not begin its metamorphosis to seed clam unless the salinity is at least eighteen to twenty parts per thousand, ensuring that the seed clam will not set in an area where the salinity is unsuitable for adults.

Clams also prefer a bottom substrate of sand or mud, and this is what the larval clam or seed clam looks for. The clam's favorite habitat is a sandy bottom in a shallow estuary where the current moves the water at a fairly leisurely pace. Clams don't like the fast-moving water of inlets, nor do they like turbid waters where the bottom has been disturbed. Although they feed on suspended food particles, excessive turbidity can clog the filtering system and eventually kill the clam.

When the seed clam finds an environment of proper salinity and with adequate food supply, it becomes a permanent resident. As the clam grows, it develops a tough muscle called a foot. The clam opens it shell, extends the foot, and uses it to dig into the substrate. The clam burrows under approximately one inch, and then extends its pair of siphons upward to draw in seawater and nutrients to expel waste.

Once the clam has found its home, it will not go far from its territory. The clam can use its foot to dig itself out and relocate, but scientists believe most adult clams stay within one square meter of their home. If the clam senses danger, such as the digging of a cow-nose ray, it will burrow deeper into the substrate until the danger passes.

As they grow, many young clams undergo a sex change. At one year old, clams are functional males, although their permanent sexual identity is not yet determined. Over the next year or two, the clams mature and become either male or female at about a one-to-one ratio.

The clam feeds by filtering phytoplankton, bacteria, detritus, and dissolved organic material from seawater through a pair of attached siphons that develop during the seed clam stage. The incurrent siphon, which brings in nutrients, has tiny tentacles along its rim that sort out possible food particles. The tentacles act as the off-on switch for the incurrent siphon. When plenty of nutrients are suspended in the current, the tentacles tell the clam to go into the feeding mode; if the seawater is clouded with suspended particles of sand, mud, and other large debris, the tentacles shut the system down.

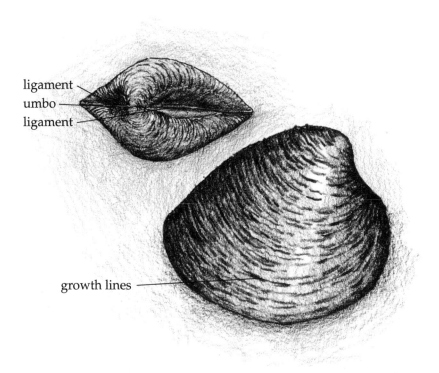

ligament
umbo
ligament

growth lines

Seawater is pumped into the clam by the gills, and food particles are attached to the gills in a thick mucus solution. Hairlike cilia on the gills move the food particles slowly toward the mouthparts, where tissues that line the entrance further sort out the food particles, deciding which will be ingested and which will be rejected. Rejected particles, called pseudofeces, are moved by cilia to the base of the siphon. When a sufficient amount of waste has been collected, it is forcibly ejected in a stream of water.

A female clam is at the peak of her sexual prowess when she is three years old and measures about sixty millimeters in length. A healthy female in the wild will release sixteen million to twenty-four million eggs during the spawning season, which on the Virginia coast runs from May through August.

In laboratory tests, large, chowder-size females have produced more than fifty million eggs per season.

Only a small percentage of the eggs survive to become adult clams. The eggs, spermatozoa, and clam larvae all become part of the zooplankton carried by the currents through the estuary, which in summer provides a nutrient-rich soup for a wide variety of animals. Scientists say that in a shallow seaside estuary during the summer months, there can be as many as thirty million clam larvae per square meter.

Most of the larvae are eaten by fish, crabs, birds, and other mollusks. Even clams eat their own eggs and larvae by filtering them out of seawater. The clam's vulnerability decreases as it outgrows the army of predators. Once the clam becomes an adult and burrows into the bottom, the predators become fairly specific. Skates, rays, and mud, blue, and green crabs dig clams out of the sediment. The crabs crush the smaller shells with their claws and chip off the edges of larger shells. When clamming on an exposed tidal flat at low tide, you can often see shallow depressions left by skates and rays, which use their wings to locate and dig out clams.

Our methods of digging clams are perhaps no more sophisticated. We look for sign of something not immediately seen, and then we dig. If we are fortunate, there will be enough clams in the basket for chowder, and we will return home weary and covered with salt spray, all the richer for having spent a day on the tidal flats, nourishing our bodies and our souls.

5   Clam Facts: A Conversation with Mike Castagna

Mike Castagna of the Virginia Institute of Marine Science (VIMS) is an expert on clams and a pioneer in the field of clam aquaculture. He has helped the clam aquaculture industry on Virginia's Eastern Shore grow to a $50 million-a-year business. But while clams have become big business, Mike's appreciation for clams goes beyond their market value. He has studied wild clams extensively and has helped countless recreational clammers become more knowledgeable. We talked about clams and clamming at the VIMS laboratory in Wachapreague, Virginia.

How far and how often do clams move?
It depends on the size. A larval clam goes all over. Then the clam develops a foot and crawls until it finds a place it likes. If it can't find a place it likes, it swims again. Finally, it metamorphoses and puts down its foot and loses the velum that it swims with.

Smaller-size clams will flush out of the bottom and let the current carry them. An experienced clammer can come into an area he's never seen before and tell you where the clams are going to be. For example, if there's a structure in the water, such as an old boat, the clams will be on the downcurrent side of it. On a turn in a channel, the clams will be on the outside of the turn. You find them where the current velocity drops below the critical velocity to carry that size clam. We didn't know this until we began planting clams and losing them. A year later, they'd show up fifty or a hundred yards away. It takes only a quarter of a knot of current to move a clam the size of a quarter.

Mature clams move very little, perhaps a meter in a week. When you go into an area and find many clams, then come back a few days later and find none, this doesn't mean the clams have left the area; it means they've gone deep. It's a response to predators.

What kind of home do clams look for?
Clams can't stand a lot of clay, but they can live in most anything else, as long as it's stable enough for them to bury and stay put. When you look at catch records, you'll find that most are caught where there are a lot of shells. On a sandy mudflat, you might get one clam in three to nine square meters. On a shell pile, you'll get as many as thirteen per square meter. It's not a matter of preference, but a matter of protection. When clams set, or put down their feet, they are smaller than one-sixteenth inch and are very vulnerable. When you see little shrimp scavenging along the bottom, they're eating clams. When clams get bigger and develop siphons, they can dig in and go deeper, but they still can be dug out by crabs, rays, and other predators. One blue crab can eat about seventy-five small clams in a night.

A worse predator is the mud crab. Blue crabs are territorial, and there usually is only one in a given area, but mud crabs can be as dense as three hundred per square meter, and each one can eat thirty-five clams between sunset and sunrise. When we first began putting out clams in beds, we found that we could put out one toadfish, a crab predator, under the net, and it would keep the crabs in check. But in the wild, shell rocks help protect clams from predators such as crabs, which would have to move the shells away to get at the clams.

If clams have no brains, how do they know to take shelter among spent shells?

They don't know at all. One female clam can produce sixty thousand eggs, which are planktonic. Larvae move with the current, as do small clams. The ones that happen to end up in a shell environment have a better chance of survival. It's purely happenstance. It's the luck of the draw.

How fast do clams grow?

A clam three or four inches in diameter would be probably three to five years old. Clams that are started in hatcheries get a little of a head start. We get them to market size in twenty-two to twenty-eight months, market size being littleneck steamers, about one and a half inches in diameter. The oldest clams we've seen have been thirty-three to thirty-six years old. The bulk of the clam predators target young clams. Cownose rays and skates like the same size clams we do, littlenecks, because they can crush the shells.

Do clams become dormant in the winter?

Clams feed year-round, though they feed less in winter because they need less energy. If the clam is happy and not threatened, it will be open and pumping all day. In winter, it's more likely to be open, because cold water carries more oxygen than warm water. When the oxygen level drops, the clam closes up. In summer, the seawater is a soup of phytoplankton and zooplankton. The plankton converts CO_2 to oxygen as soon as it gets sunlight. So the oxygen level goes up sharply from dawn until about 8 or 10 A.M., and then levels off. After sundown, the plankton become inactive, and the oxygen level drops precipitously. Once it gets below about two milligrams per liter, the clams close up. Thus in winter, the clams might stay open twenty-four hours a day, and in summer, they close at night.

When opening clams, I've found things that look like worms and small leeches. Are these parasites?

The tubular, wormlike structure is actually part of the clam, called the crystalline stile. It's a clear tube that is slightly tapered, and it has to do with the digestive system.

The small, flat organisms you might find are clam leeches. They're not harmful to humans. If you eat fifty steamed clams, chances are you'll eat one or two clam leeches.

How has the clam aquaculture industry on the Eastern Shore grown, and what is its economic impact?

The aquaculture clam industry generates about $50 million a year on the Eastern Shore, and it is still growing. It employs about three hundred people, many of whom are watermen who would not be employed on the water if it were not for aquaculture. There are all sorts of related opportunities. We helped a company in North Carolina develop a dig-your-own-clam business. They buy Eastern Shore clams, put them out on their bottom, and charge tourists to dig them. One of the guys told me they're making a fortune selling "I dug my own" T-shirts. A business like that should certainly do well on the shore, especially in an area such as Chincoteague.

6   How to Cook Clams

M any veteran clammers will tell you that when it comes
to eating clams, less is more. I've seen old-time clammers, on lunch break, open a couple dozen samples from
the morning catch and have them with saltines and iced tea.
"I can feel his heart beat on my tongue," a clammer once
told me.

The problem with eating raw clams is that clams are filter
feeders, and unless you know that the water they were taken
from is clean, you stand a very good chance of picking up a
nasty illness. Local health departments monitor waterways
for contaminants, such as fecal coliform bacteria, but when
you buy clams on the open market, you have no guarantee
where they came from. There are too many wonderful ways
to cook clams to take a chance of becoming ill by eating raw
shellfish.

Along the Atlantic coast, perhaps the favorite way of eating clams is steamed and dipped in a little melted butter.
The clams used for steaming are small. Littlenecks have a
diameter of about an inch and a half. Cherrystones are somewhat larger. Both are wonderful steamed, tender and flavorful, with a salty bite that reminds you of the seaside.

Larger clams are a bit tough for steaming but are perfect
for making fritters, chowder, pie, or sauce to serve over pasta.
Purists argue that clams should be chopped coarsely with a
chef's knife, never minced in a food processor. I once agreed,
but I've found that I can chop them perfectly in a food processor if I don't overdo it. Just a few pulses are all that's needed,

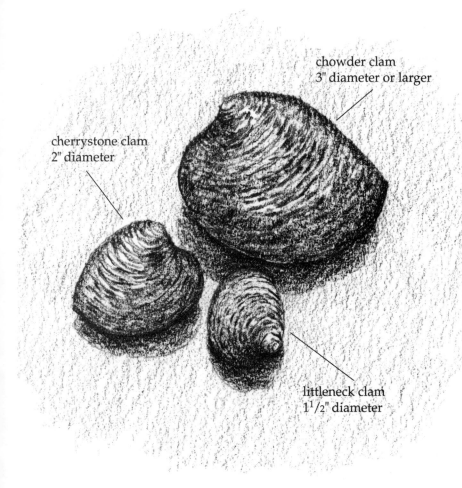

chowder clam
3" diameter or larger

cherrystone clam
2" diameter

littleneck clam
$1^1/_2$" diameter

with careful monitoring between pulses. For me, the processor is much quicker and easier than the knife.

People who live near the coast are familiar with recipes using fresh clams recently removed from the shell, such as steamed clams, linguine with clam sauce, fried whole clams, clam fritters, clam pie, and clam chowder. Travel inland a bit, mention clams, and people think of fried clam strips and canned clam chowder. In most cases, these are made from surf or sea clams, *Spissula solidissima*, or ocean clams, *Arctica islandica.* These large clams live in offshore waters, where they are dredged by oceangoing vessels and shipped to mainland processing plants. Approximately 2,565,000 bushels of sea clams and 4,200,000 bushels of ocean clams are harvested from federal waters annually. The clams are processed as soup and chowder, clam strips, clam cakes, and clam juice.

I do not mean to disparage offshore clams, and I realize that *Mercenaria* are difficult to come by in, let's say, Toledo, so I would not want to deny Toledoans their processed strips and chowder at the Friday evening seafood buffet. I wish, however, that I could favor each of them with a dozen little-necks with butter, followed by a bowl of Cedar Island clam chowder made from clams taken from a tidal flat about an hour before dinner.

The subject of chowder causes clammers to swell with regional pride. Most of us know that New England chowder is rich and creamy, whereas Manhattan chowder is light and has a tomato base. At least, that's the generalization perpetuated by those who sell canned clam chowder.

But there are hundreds, probably thousands, of versions of clam chowder, with the followers of each acting like flag-waving generals from tiny republics, demanding to be heard and recognized. It goes far beyond creamy versus tomato-based.

On the Virginia coast, one of the favorites is called Hog Island clam chowder, a recipe that dates back to the village of Broadwater, which until the 1930s was a thriving island village of some 250 souls. Broadwater succumbed to a rising sea level, and many of the homes and stores were barged to the mainland, but Hog Island chowder lives on, served with pride by local residents who have family ties to the island.

Hog Island clam chowder is a simple concoction of fresh, coarsely chopped clams, potatoes fried in bacon grease, and a few onions and chopped tomatoes. The tomatoes are kept to a minimum, however; this is not a "tomato-based" chowder.

Purists insist that a true "Eastern Shore" clam chowder should consist only of potatoes, chopped clams with their juice, and a little black pepper. A tomato never befouls this chowder, nor does cream.

Most clam chowder recipes begin with a combination of clams, potatoes, and onions. Beyond that, anything goes. A recipe that follows, courtesy of Flounders Restaurant, uses thyme and oregano as seasoning agents. Some chowder enthusiasts like the fire of cayenne pepper or Old Bay seasoning. Mace is an ingredient in some recipes.

My favorite chowder recipe at the moment is called Cedar Island clam chowder because that's where I catch most of my clams. This recipe goes against the grain somewhat, in that it has more than the average number of ingredients; it flies in the face of the "less is more" theory. I like it because it is an interesting blend of flavors. It uses garlic and fresh parsley, which go nicely with clams in linguine, and a dash of mace, which many clam pie recipes call for. The final ingredient is a bit of half-and-half (fat free, if you insist), which makes the chowder appear creamy. But it's not New England. The recipe appears later in this chapter, so you can judge for yourself.

Opening Clams

I went to a watermen's festival recently, and one of the exhibits featured a group of workers from a seafood packing house demonstrating the art of opening a clam. Most of the workers were women, and they would pick up a clam, rake the bill—the front edge of the clam—across a coarse rasp mounted on their table, and insert a sturdy knife through the opening created by the rasp. The women then worked the knife back and forth quickly, severing both adductor muscles, and the clam would open in a cascade of salt water. The entire process took only a few seconds.

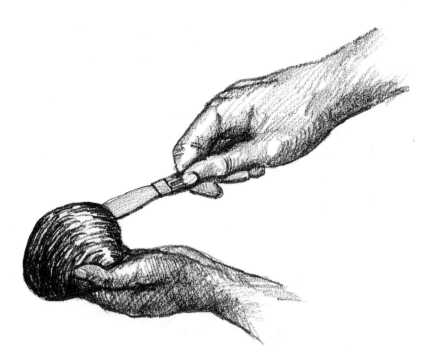

My father used a similar technique. He kept a cinder block by the back porch, and when he had a mess of clams to open, he sat on the back steps with the cinder block by his side. He would scrape the bill of the clam across the block a few times, insert an oyster knife into the opening, and before long, the soft, orange flesh of the clam would be shimmering in a quart jar. The neighborhood cats would gather to lap up the spilled clam juice.

Another method of opening a clam is to insert a slim-bladed oyster knife just above the hinge on the back of the clamshell. This tiny spot is the only place where the shell is vulnerable. Once the blade is inserted, move it back and forth to sever the adductor muscles, and then the two shells can be easily separated.

The only drawback to these three methods is that there is something inherently dangerous about combining knives and clamshells. I've seen too many pierced palms, and I have on occasion donated blood of my own.

The easiest and safest way to open clams is to put them in the freezer. After an hour or so, they will open with relative ease. Keep them in the freezer overnight, and by the next morning they will be open. Thaw them and add them to your favorite recipe.

The freezer method of opening clams has several advantages, other than safety. You will not likely encounter shell fragments in your linguine, which happens from time to time with the scrape and stick method. Also, freezing allows you to retain all of that flavorful, salty clam juice, and this can be both good and bad. Clam juice is too tasty to have it run down the drain or be lapped up by cats. But it is very salty, which can be an issue if you or a dinner guest has high blood pressure. I once made linguine with clam sauce using only the

clams' own juice, and I reduced the sauce for far too long, resulting in a salty broth that was inedible. I've since learned to combine the clam juice with low-fat, low salt chicken stock.

Clams can also be opened by steaming them open, and in recipes such as clam risotto, which calls for littleneck clams in the shell, this method is perfect. The problem with steaming is that in doing so, you are cooking the clam, and that wonderful juice is being diluted with the cooking water. In some recipes, this doesn't matter, but when making chowder, clam pie, linguine with clam sauce, or fritters, I prefer to begin with a raw clam in its own juices.

Clam Recipes
What follows is an eclectic mix of clam recipes. Some of these are mine, and others have been generously donated by friends. When cooking clams, I urge you to experiment. Clams are a wonderfully versatile seafood, and their flavor complements so many other foods and spices. When you consider a chowder recipe, think beyond creamy or tomato.

Cedar Island Clam Chowder

Ingredients
15 to 18 large chowder clams with juice
6 medium potatoes, peeled and cubed
1 medium onion, chopped
about 1 tablespoon bacon grease
4 to 6 garlic cloves
1 cup low-fat chicken stock
1 carrot
1 cup half-and-half
ground black pepper to taste
mace
a few sprigs of fresh parsley

Directions
1. Sauté the cubed potatoes and onion in the bacon grease until a glaze forms on the bottom of the pan and the potatoes and onion are lightly browned.
2. Chop the garlic and lightly brown it with the potatoes and onion.
3. Deglaze the pan with clam juice and chicken stock.
4. Shred the carrot and add to the chowder.
5. Coarsely chop the clams and add to the pot with black pepper, parsley, and a dash of mace.
6. Let simmer until potatoes are done and chowder has thickened.
7. Add a cup of half-and-half, stir, and serve.

Hurley's Clam Chowder

Flounders Restaurant, Onancock, Virginia

Ingredients
about 2 dozen medium clams, coarsely chopped, with juice
3 cups water
$1/8$ pound bacon
$1/4$ cup onion, chopped
3 stalks celery, diced
1 large green bell pepper, chopped
1 large can whole tomatoes
1 teaspoon oregano
1 teaspoon thyme
$1/2$ teaspoon ground black pepper
2 pounds potatoes, diced

Directions
1. Simmer the bacon, onion, celery, green pepper, and tomatoes in 3 cups of water.
2. In a separate pot, simmer the chopped clams in their juice with the oregano, thyme, and black pepper.
3. Combine all ingredients, add the diced potatoes, and simmer another half hour.

Linguine with Clam Sauce

Ingredients
about a dozen large clams, coarsely chopped, with liquid
1 tablespoon olive oil
3 or 4 garlic cloves, chopped
linguine
fresh parsley
black pepper

Directions
1. Sauté garlic in olive oil until golden.
2. Add chopped clams with liquid, and cook until clams are done.
3. Meanwhile, prepare pasta according to instructions on container.
4. Add pepper to taste.
5. Chop parsley and sprinkle over clam sauce.
6. Spoon sauce over linguine, and serve with garlic bread or bruschetta.

Note: This recipe uses clam liquid and is quite salty. To reduce the salt content, replace half of the clam juice with low-fat, low-salt chicken stock.

Clam Fritters

Terry Swain, Hunting Creek, Virginia

Ingredients
12 to 18 large clams, shucked and coarsely chopped
black pepper
1 egg
$^1/_2$ cup flour
$1^1/_2$ teaspoons baking powder
$^1/_2$ teaspoon baking soda
1 medium onion, diced
cooking oil

Directions
1. Mix well the first seven ingredients.
2. Heat about $^1/_2$ inch oil in skillet.
3. Spoon mixture into hot oil to make fritters about 4 inches in diameter.
4. Cook on one side until golden brown, then turn.
5. Drain fritters on paper towels before serving.

Clam Pie

Ingredients
about a dozen large clams, opened and coarsely chopped
1 egg
3 tablespoons evaporated milk
1 cup bread crumbs
1 medium onion, chopped
1 teaspoon Worcestershire sauce
2 tablespoons melted butter
$^1/_4$ green bell pepper, chopped

Directions
1. Preheat oven to 400° F.
2. Mix the above ingredients, and pour into a lightly greased pie plate.
3. Bake for about 30 minutes.

Folly Creek Clam Pie

Ingredients

    12 to 15 large clams with juice, opened and coarsely
       chopped
    2 medium potatoes, cubed
    1 stalk celery, chopped
    1 carrot, grated
    1 cup low-fat, low-salt chicken stock
    2 tablespoons fresh parsley, chopped
    6 ounces evaporated milk
    black pepper to taste
    dash of mace
    1 tablespoon butter
    2 tablespoons flour
    2 frozen pie crusts, thawed

Directions

1. Cook potatoes, celery, and carrots in clam juice and chicken stock until tender, adding water if necessary to cover.
2. Add parsley, milk, black pepper, and mace. Make a roux by melting butter in a small saucepan and slowly adding flour while stirring. Add flour until the texture becomes pastelike and cook until light brown. Add the roux to the mixture to thicken.
3. Simmer 10 to 15 minutes to reduce volume.
4. While liquid is cooking, place one pie crust in the bottom of a glass pie plate.

(continued)

5. Add chopped clams to the mixture and cook until done, about 10 minutes.
6. Use a slotted spoon to transfer the clam mixture to the pie plate. Save excess liquid to use as gravy.
7. Place second crust on top of filled pie plate, tucking edges of the top layer under edges of the bottom layer. Seal edges by pressing them together with a fork. Use a knife to cut four 1-inch vents in top crust.
8. Bake at 425° F for 15 minutes, then reduce heat to 350° and bake for 25 more minutes, or until crust is golden brown.

Clams Risotto

Ingredients

about a dozen large clams, coarsely chopped

18 littleneck clams in shells

12 medium shrimp, peeled

2 medium calimari, cleaned, rinsed and cut into $^1/_4$-inch rings

1 tablespoon olive oil

a few drops dark sesame oil

$^1/_2$ cup sherry

1 teaspoon each curry powder and Adobo seasoning

ground black pepper to taste

2 tablespoons roasted red peppers, coarsely chopped

2 tablespoons fresh parsley, chopped

Parmesan or Romano cheese

2 tablespoons low-fat sour cream

1 package risotto

low-fat chicken stock

Directions

1. Prepare risotto according to package directions, using chicken stock instead of water.
2. While the risotto is cooking, heat olive oil with a few drops of sesame oil in a heavy skillet, add chopped clams, shrimp, and calimari and sauté over medium high heat.
3. Add sherry, curry powder, Adobo, ground black pepper, and littleneck clams.

(continued)

4. Cover and heat until seafood is cooked through and littleneck clams have opened, about 10 minutes.
5. Add roasted red peppers and parsley, and sprinkle with Parmesan or Romano cheese
6. Remove from heat, add sour cream, and stir until sauce is smooth. Serve over risotto.

Note: Various types of seafood can be used with this recipe. The shrimp can be replaced with scallops. Crabmeat can be added. A can of smoked oysters will add a different twist to the flavor. For a nice presentation, make a ring around the edges of a shallow bowl with the risotto, and add black beans in the center. Top with the seafood mixture. If you use canned black beans, rinse them in a colander before serving, and season them with a little cumin and/or honey mustard barbecue sauce.

Deviled Clams

Ingredients

about a dozen large clams, opened and coarsely chopped
3 tablespoons evaporated milk
1 cup bread crumbs
1 small onion, chopped
1 tablespoon fresh parsley, chopped
1 teaspoon Worcestershire sauce
2 tablespoons melted butter
$1/4$ medium green pepper, chopped
dash Tabasco sauce
$1/2$ teaspoon mustard

Directions

1. Preheat oven to 400° F.
2. Mix the ingredients well, and spoon into a lightly greased pie plate or several large, washed clamshells.
3. Bake for 30 minutes.

Clams According to Bessie Gunter

In 1889 Bessie E. Gunter, a member of a prominent Accomack County family on Virginia's Eastern Shore, published a book titled *Housekeeper's Companion,* which became popularly known as the "Bessie Gunter cookbook." The book today is highly sought by collectors, not only because of its rarity, but also because it gives a glimpse of how people prepared food more than a century ago.

Recipes are those of the author and nearly one hundred other contributors, most of whom lived on the Eastern Shore. Not surprisingly, there are many recipes for oysters, clams, terrapin, fish, crabs, and other seafood. Here are two especially interesting clam recipes taken from the cookbook.

Clam Chowder

Mrs. Thos. E. C. Custis, Onancock, Virginia

Ingredients
30 clams, opened and chopped fine
2 nice size potatoes, cut in blocks
a slice of pork, cut as the potatoes
1 pint of tomatoes
1 onion, cut fine
$1/2$ pint milk or cream
butter the size of an egg
pepper
thyme

(continued)

Directions

1. Put the first five ingredients on to cook in about a pint of water.
2. Boil a half hour or longer, then add a little pepper, milk or cream, and butter.
3. Don't let it boil too dry; it should be the consistency of vegetable soup when done.
4. Season with a little thyme and serve hot.

Scalloped Clams

Miss Corson, no address given

Ingredients
    3 dozen large hardshell clams
    1 medium onion, peeled and chopped
    2 tablespoons butter
    2 tablespoons flour
    1 cup milk or cream
    $1/4$ teaspoon nutmeg
    as much cayenne pepper as can be taken up on the point of
        a small knife blade
    6 egg yolks

Directions
1. Wash the shells of the three dozen clams and put them over the fire in a saucepan with a close cover until the shells open.
2. Fry the onion in the butter until it is light brown.
3. Remove the clams from the shells and chop fine.
4. When the onion is light brown, add the flour, then the clams and the milk or cream.
5. Season with the nutmeg and cayenne pepper.
6. Stew the clams gently for half an hour.
7. Meanwhile, arrange the washed clam shells on a dripping pan.
8. When the clams are done, remove the saucepan from the fire, stir in the yolks of six raw eggs, and put this mixture into the clam shells.

(continued)

9. Set them in a very hot oven until they are slightly browned, and serve them very hot.

Note: You can experiment with this Civil War–era recipe by adding various toppings before browning the clams, such as crumbled bacon or chopped spinach and feta cheese.

7   Clam Boats

M y clam boat is a sixteen-foot Polar Kraft aluminum johnboat that I consider an army jeep for the water. Its color is fatigue green, faded, not crisp. It has scars here and there where the aluminum shows through. Some have been touched up, but the paint doesn't quite match, giving the boat a somewhat camouflaged look.

When I bought the boat, the bottom had aluminum ribs every sixteen inches, making it difficult to walk around without tripping over a rib. So I bought some sheets of plastic insulation from my local building supply store and cut them to fit between the ribs. Then I put half-inch plywood on top of the ribs and plastic, and screwed it down with stainless steel sheet metal screws. I painted the plywood fatigue green to almost match the aluminum.

The boat has a twenty-five-horsepower outboard motor. It doesn't have a steering wheel, a compass, or a radio. It is a no-nonsense clam boat, and I start it by pulling a starting rope and steer it by pushing and pulling the tiller back and forth. If I get in shallow water, which I often do when searching for clams, I tilt the motor out of the water and propel the boat with a push-pole. I made one from a twelve-foot piece of closet rod purchased at a building-supply store. On one end I fastened a gadget called a "duck bill," which opens up when you push it into soft mud, providing some resistance. I painted the push-pole fatigue green.

My boat doesn't sound like much, does it? I'll tell you what—if I had all the money in the world, I wouldn't buy

anything different. Most people, when they buy a boat, use it for six weeks and wish they had something larger, or faster, or sleeker. Not me. You can bury me with my clam boat. I decided to name my clam boat shortly after I bought it. My first thought was to name it for my wife, but I decided she'd probably be insulted. So I named it *Mercenaria,* the Latin name for the hardshell clam. I like the name. It's appropriate for the boat's duty in life, and it has a certain mysterious quality. Most people don't know what *Mercenaria* means. Maybe they think I'm an agent of a third-world government.

My clam boat is about substance rather than style. It's about function rather than form. It's a throwback to the days of my father and grandfather, when boats were made in the backyards of local craftsmen, whose style was their signature. Those boats were made of eastern white cedar and were meant to do a particular job in a particular place. Here on the Virginia coast, where shallow bays separate the mainland from the barrier islands, the boats were made to have shoal drafts, flat bottoms. "You could float her on a heavy dew," a waterman once said of his clam boat.

I've clammed from canoes and from large motorboats, but I've found the johnboat to be ideal, at least until someone in the neighborhood begins making white cedar clamming boats again. It's stable, light enough to push off a sandbar at low tide, tough enough to survive scraping an oyster rock, and ugly enough that I don't have to worry about getting it dirty and dented.

I like the feel of steering the boat from the tiller, which is where small boats were meant to be steered. At some time in the past, perhaps in the forties, boat builders began making small boats that looked like cars, with steering wheels, radios, windshields, cigarette lighters, horns, lights, and glove compartments. In the fifties, boats even had tail fins.

My clam boat has none of the above, but at full throttle, it cuts a nice figure on the still waters of Folly Creek. Only about three feet of stern are in the water; the bow seems to levitate, gliding just above the surface, while the stern parts the top

few inches of the creek, sending a gentle, white-topped wake rolling toward the salt marsh on the creek shore.

When I'm not clamming, when the tide has covered the sandy flats where the clams have burrowed, I explore the marsh with the clam boat. Folly Creek is the main drag here, with a public boat ramp and all the traffic that comes with it. I get off the main drag and onto side streets with colorful names like Knockknees Gut, Piggin Gut, Teagle's Ditch, and Longboat Creek. Many of these little waterways are not on the nautical charts; their names have been passed down from generation to generation, and no one knows for sure how they got them.

Knockknees winds through the marsh like a mountain road, all switchbacks and hairpins, and a local waterman tells me if you go fast enough through Knockknees, you can meet yourself coming the other way. Traveling through Knockknees in a small motorboat, then, is like testing the theory of relativity. If we go fast enough, we can go back in time.

I like it quiet when I'm in the marsh, and I like exploring silently in my canoe. But I find a deliciously guilty sense of excitement in running at speed through Knockknees in my clam boat. The gut is narrow and lined with cordgrass, which my wake causes to dance merrily. The nearness of the grass increases the sense of speed, which, in reality, if I had a speedometer, is probably not all that great. In winter, I terrorize dozing black ducks; they rise in pairs or in groups of a half dozen, their white underwings catching the light of the low sun. They quack. I can see their bills move. Often they'll relieve themselves as they take flight, lightening the load.

Knockknees was probably named for the physical condition in which one's knees are bent toward each other. Just as the waters of Knockknees Gut are bent toward themselves.

In the taxonomy of the seaside, bodies of water are classified according to size. A creek is a substantial and well-traveled body of water. A gut is smaller, a winding, twisting, tidal stream that wanders through the marsh toward the mainland, reducing itself in size as it does. When it narrows to only a foot or two in width, it is called a drain, which is pronounced "dreen." A ditch is an unnatural body of water, created by humans.

Teagle's Ditch, then, was probably dug by, or for, someone named Teagle. A search of the local phone book yields no one by that name on the Eastern Shore of Virginia. Teagle's Ditch is a narrow passage between two salt marsh meadows and is part of the Virginia Inside Passage of the Intracoastal Waterway. When the VIP was dug, perhaps Teagle was at the controls of the dragline. Or perhaps, to add color and tragedy to our story, Teagle, a member of the crew, perished in a violent storm while attempting to secure the dragline. I'll take my cap off next time I go through Teagle's Ditch.

8   Clamming with Brant

Mudflats and oyster rocks pockmark Burton's Bay on the ebbing tide, luring all sorts of creatures, not all of which are looking for clams. In winter, the shallow waters hold great rafts of brant, their white rumps glistening in the sun as the birds tip up to eat underwater grasses. Brant to me are symbolic of the salt marsh in winter, for reasons I'm not sure I comprehend. The brant is a dark, stocky sea goose with a black head, neck, and breast, with whitish hashmarks on the sides of the neck. Its flanks are gray-brown and mottled, and its rump is white. It simply looks right here in the seaside salt marsh in winter; its colors complement those of the winter marsh. The flanks are the color of decaying *Spartina* grass, the breast and neck are the color of the exposed flat, and the white rump could be a chunk of salt ice pushed up during a hard freeze.

Beyond the color scheme, brant seem fitting and proper here in winter, especially if the sky is gray and there's a good breeze carrying a hint of snow. Then the brant will hang along the horizon in dark, irregular strings, flying low over the bays that separate the barrier islands from the mainland. If they come upon a fellow group feeding in the shallows, they will circle and come upwind, cup their wings to grab air, reduce speed, and fall gracefully one by one, barking like puppies in what must be some sort of brant greeting.

The brant's high-pitched call also seems appropriate in the winter marsh. It's a feminine version of the call of the Canada goose, softer, gentler, more melodic, and—to my ear—much wilder. Perhaps the Canada goose has become too familiar

where we live here on the Virginia coast. They are on people's lawns, on golf courses, in community parks and ponds. They have become commonplace and no longer wild. The brant, however, is a loner; it doesn't associate with people. If you want to see and hear them you have to get out here on the bays and marshes in winter, when the wind is blowing and the temperature makes it tempting to stay at home by the fire. There will be thousands of them by late December, especially if the weather has been harsh up north. They will stay until March or so, and then begin their long flight north to their breeding grounds in the Arctic.

The winter marsh is a wild place. Most of the people who live here on the coast have put their boats away for the winter, and on most days there is no one around, none of the sights and sounds of civilization, and so the wilderness aspects of the landscape are heightened. Brant are part of this. They, too, are wild, and they belong especially to this singular place. I can remember seeing them in a mainland farm field only once, during a winter in which a hard freeze covered the bays with ice, starving the brant, which feed on submerged vegetation. They had taken refuge in a field of winter wheat, feeding there with Canada geese, black ducks, mallards, and snow geese. The brant seemed emphatically out of place.

Clamming in winter is an excuse to get out where the brant are. On a raw day in January, it's difficult to explain to your family that you want to take the boat out and listen to the brant. Instead, I put it in terms of clams. "Some hot clam chowder sure would be good on a day like today."

The mention of clam chowder in winter tickles more senses than that of taste. We heat our house with wood, and the stove is in the basement where my office is. When I make chowder, I begin it in the morning on the gas range in the kitchen, sautéing potatoes and garlic in a small amount of bacon grease, and then adding a cup or so of chicken broth and cooking the potatoes until they are tender. And then the chopped clams and clam juice go in, with some chopped parsley, a cup of half-and-half, and a hint of mace, and the pot is removed to the woodstove in my office, where the aroma rises with the heat to the upper two floors of our house, suffusing all with the daylong hope that dinner will be early.

And so, with memories of chowders past, it seems totally logical to break out the little johnboat on a frigid day, to pull on the thermals and the wool sweater, the waterproof jacket, and the hipboots. The running time to the clamming flats is perhaps fifteen minutes, the coldest part of the trip. Once the boat is beached, once I am on the flat, bent at the waist, pecking the surface with my clam pick, it no longer seems cold.

The boat surprised the brant when I went out, but once I reached the flat, I became in their minds just another creature looking for a meal. They foraged in the shallow waters off the edge of the flat, barking softly as they fed, as loose strings of brant came from over the barrier island and joined them.

9 Clamming by Land

Bellevue Farm is owned by The Nature Conservancy, which gives me permission to hike there in exchange for keeping an eye on the place. It is one of the few places I can go clamming without using the boat. Bellevue is a seaside farm, a mix of pine woods, farm fields, and salt marsh that stretches for more than a mile along the shores of Burton's Bay and Finney Creek. A peninsula of marsh and forest is created where the creek empties into the bay, and a woods road runs from the farm fields all the way to the tip of the peninsula, a distance of about a half mile.

A tidal flat lies at the tip of the peninsula, no doubt created by silt having been washed down Finney Creek in innumerable ebb tides, and slowly deposited here off my wooded point where the velocity of the current would slow as the creek enters Burton's Bay. At low tide, I can walk through the marsh and to the flat, where I can sign clams while the bottom is exposed.

I try to make the trip once or twice each spring. In March, we begin to get visitors from the south, and I enjoy meeting them on my way to the clamming flats. I am speaking of birds, specifically warblers that spent the winter in Central America and now are on their way to the northern United States and Canada to raise a new brood.

Pine warblers are among the first to come through. I hear them in the tops of the loblolly pines along the woods road, their song a long, steady trill. Soon prairie warblers will come, and northern parulas, black-throated greens, and worm-eating

warblers, as well as other songbirds such as tanagers and thrushes. They will replace the yellow-rumped warblers that spent the winter in these woods, feeding on the little blue berries of wax myrtles and cedars.

I hike through the woods carrying a clam basket and pick, binoculars hanging around my neck, and I stop often to catch a glimpse of a songbird in the treetops. Recently I heard a prairie warbler—its song is similar to that of the pine warbler, but with an ascending note at the end—and I stood still and made a "pishing" sound, forcing air out between clenched teeth.

Soon I saw the bird in the myrtle thicket, glittering like gold in the sun. I "pished" again and it came closer, perching on the limb of a wild black cherry perhaps ten feet in front of me. It was a beautiful little bird, a male in full breeding plumage, with a bright yellow breast and face, dark eyeline, and dark specks along its flanks. It regarded me with curiosity, leaning forward, turning its head side to side. After a few seconds, it decided I was not a threat or a rival for its territory, and off it went.

I enjoy these clamming trips because of the birds, and I realize they are the reason I go, not necessarily the clams. Indeed, we have clams in the freezer, and my need to gather more has nothing to do with greed or hunger, but with the desire to get out in the woods on a spring day and meet these migrants, most of which will be with us for only a few weeks.

I also enjoy the irony of clamming with spring warblers. On most clamming trips, I share a tidal flat with gulls, terns, willets, plovers, whimbrels, and other shorebirds and wading birds. It's not often I'm face-to-face with a prairie warbler when I go clamming.

I hike through the woods, step out onto the salt marsh, cross a shallow drain, and am on the tidal flat. There's a breeze out here, carrying with it the remnants of winter. Cormorants forage in the shallow bay east of the flat, and in the distance, over Cedar Island, I see a flock of black ducks flying north, their light gray underwings catching the sun.

It's a half hour past low tide, and the clams are signing nicely. In a sandy edge sculpted by the tide, I find large ones, with spattering of water around the siphon holes. I need only a dozen or so of these for dinner. I've been experimenting with a Civil War–era recipe for scalloped clams, and this is what I'll try tonight. I'll chop the clams, cook them in their broth, and add some flour, seasonings, and cream. When they're done, I'll add egg yolks to thicken the mixture, then spoon it into large clamshells and broil it. That's what the old recipe calls for. But I want to try something different. I'll top it with chopped spinach and feta before broiling.

On the way back, the warblers are still singing, staking claim to territory, luring mates. A few will spend the summer here, but most will continue northward, traveling this wooded corridor all the way up the coast. And then in fall they'll return, stopping in these woods to refuel during their trip to the tropics. I'll be here with my clam pick and basket, ready to greet them.